I CAN'T READ

I ~~CAN'T~~ READ

A Guide to Success Through Failure

WILLIAM MANZANARES IV

LIONCREST
PUBLISHING

I CAN'T READ
A Guide to Success Through Failure

ISBN	978-1-5445-1416-1	*Hardcover*
	978-1-5445-1415-4	*Paperback*
	978-1-5445-1414-7	*Ebook*
	978-1-5445-0358-5	*Audiobook*

This book is dedicated to Karisi. Papa loves you and will never forget the impact you made on his life. May this book have an impact on many more lives because of you.

CONTENTS

INTRODUCTION

B.G. had been living at a homeless shelter when we met.

One of my employees volunteered there. When B.G. found out where he worked, he began showing up to one of my businesses, offering to help however he could. My employees gave him money or bought him things to eat, though he never expected any of it in return.

I hadn't heard about him until it came to my attention that one of my employees abused his generous nature, taking advantage by having him pick up garbage without offering him anything. I was less than happy with that fact, so the next day, I introduced myself to B.G. I liked him immediately, and we got to know each other well.

Never so well, though, as on a short road trip we took together.

I'd rented a truck to move some equipment for one of my businesses and asked B.G., along with another employee, to help. During the drive, I told my employee about how I wanted to write a book for people with reading difficulties. I told them that I was bouncing around the idea of "I Can't Read" for a title. At that moment, B.G. piped up from the back seat. His eyes were lit up with excitement.

"I'd read that book, Will," he said. "Because I can't read."

I was shocked. I decided to test him—not because I didn't believe him, but because I wanted to see exactly what he meant by saying he was unable to read—to see if it meant the same thing to me as it did to him. I pointed out street signs and billboards as we drove. He sounded them out, most with only a small amount of difficulty. We then approached a sign for a street named Weyerhauser Way. I knew people who could read who struggled pronouncing that one. Even though he had to sound it out slowly and deliberately, he was able to say it. I was amazed.

"Whoa, wait a minute," I said. "Who told you that you couldn't read?"

He talked about taking an aptitude test at a point in his life that had to do with his present situation. While the circumstances of that time aren't important, what is important are the results. He failed a standardized test that identified him as one of the millions of people in our country unable to read, even though he showed with the signs that he clearly could.

I told him so, but he didn't believe it, or wouldn't, so I decided to tell him something else.

"There's a specific reason I'm writing this book," I said. He guessed that it was because I was a successful businessman who wanted to pass on that success to others.

"No, B.G.," I said. "You can do what I can't. You can see letters and use them to sound out words. I can't read."

A SHARED STRUGGLE

If you're reading this book, chances are you have someone in your life who has some kind of difficulty with reading. The problem is, you might not know it. For whatever reason, those who can't read find ways to hide it. They avoid reading in public or invent strategies to memorize words by sight, anything to keep anyone from finding out the truth about their challenges.

Maybe you know but have struggled with how to help. Maybe you have reading difficulties, too, and don't know how to help your loved ones without first helping yourself.

No matter who you are, no matter if these challenges are yours or belong to someone you care about, you probably feel alone. You might feel like no one understands how hard it is for you to watch your sons or daughters or partners suffer with this condition.

You are not alone.

I'm going to tell you the story of a young boy who discovered at a very early age that he couldn't read. I'm going to tell you how he learned to reframe his condition and developed strategies well into adulthood that turned him into the successful independent business owner he is today.

I'm going to tell you about me.

I'm going to tell you about my path of self-discovery in the hopes that you will find some inspiration in my struggle. I understand those feelings of fear, frustration, and embarrassment associated with illiteracy.

I've experienced the frustration of looking at a word and having no idea what it was. I've lived in fear of having to read something in a public setting or a classroom.

I've been there. Not only that, I'm here to tell you that with work, with a shift in mind frame about reading disabilities, success is possible.

WHAT YOU WILL LEARN

There is hope.

There is hope because of technology. There is hope because the people who suffered reading disabilities before these advances in technology existed had a hand in creating them.

You will learn the importance of reframing the struggle to read in a positive light. You will learn how to see it as a superpower—or a path to developing one—instead of thinking of it as a hindrance to your success.

As a parent, you will learn how you must never make excuses for your child, neither for their disability nor for their avoiding the work it takes to overcome it. When you reveal their struggle, you will discover that you and your child aren't always supported. There will always be those who look down on their disability, both children and adults. Not everyone will be an ally.

In realizing that, you'll be able to take from this book how to be the best team member possible, to help them push through the difficult times, and how to get them excited about reading by giving the act purpose.

You'll learn all this from stories from my own personal journey, both the highs and the lows, from my past challenges to the methods and tools I use to this day.

WHY NOW?

From the second I told more than three people in my life about my struggle, I have discovered a number of things. While many of them gave me the motivation to write this book, there is one that stands out more than any other. This last is the most important motivation of them all but more on that later.

So many who share this struggle with reading don't want to share their story. As a result, they suffer alone.

No more.

When I revealed my truth to my employees, the reactions were not what I expected. Those results drove me to research the amount of illiteracy in our country, and the discovery that it is as common, if not more so, than some of the worst diseases in history was shocking to me. Worst of all, no one is talking about it in a real and personal way.

No more.

I decided to stand up for those who can't because they don't know how, and for those who won't because they think it's impossible. While I've found solutions to my own disability, I am no more special than you, your child, or anyone who shares this challenge. Like I did, anyone with the willingness to put in the work can make reading easier.

BE WARNED

If you bought this book expecting an academic review of why reading struggles are what they are and how they have gotten as bad as they have, then you should stop now. If you are looking for an in-depth explanation and examination of illiteracy in our country, you have come to the wrong place.

This book is not about the root causes of reading disabilities.

It is also not a quick fix. If you've purchased this for someone in your life or for yourself, expecting that you will solve reading challenges overnight, you are in for a disappointment.

I am no expert, and don't claim to be one. The methods I have used to tackle my personal challenges have no scientific evidence stating they are the most effective or useful. However, they have proven effective for me, and I owe it to those who experience the same or similar struggle to share my story and strategies with them.

This book is a story told through the eyes of one person who struggled and the people he met along the way who lived that struggle with him. It's for those who don't have difficulty reading to understand what it's like to live with these challenges, and how to recognize it in someone who might be hiding it from you. It's about helping you nurture the goals of a child and finding ways to help them achieve them.

Make no mistake: this will be a difficult journey. Just because someone makes the decision to improve their reading doesn't mean things automatically get easier. You will struggle to understand your child's frustration, and it will be hard to control your own. You will test your patience, as well as theirs. There will be low times, and there will be tears.

I know, though, that if this book can provide just one useful tool, one story that provides inspiration to take action, then the promise I made to finish this for you and those you love will all be worth it.

WHERE IT ALL BEGAN

Every journey begins with the first step. Mine began in the second grade.

Let's take a step backwards to that time in my life, so that we can move forward to the other side together.

Chapter One

THE STRUGGLE BEGINS

I first realized I had a problem in the second grade, when my teacher moved me back to first grade reading. It was terrifying. You're the oldest kid in the group. Every grade counts when you're that age, and now I'm being moved to a class below me. Even there amongst the first graders, I continued to struggle. Most of them were reading better than I was.

I recall that at times during first-grade reading, during the holidays, we would give up completing our reading assignments for arts and crafts time. This is to say we weren't always reading. It was a way for my struggle with it to fly under the radar, so much so that I was able to reach the third grade without having actually gone through second-grade reading. The fact upset my third-grade teacher. She once asked the class to praise Pancho—my family nickname at the time—as I struggled through a class reading. She said to them:

"He's doing really well. He skipped second-grade reading. You all had it and he didn't, and he's still doing well."

I hadn't realized that it was a big deal to skip second-grade reading. She tried to explain to the class that I was struggling because I had skipped it. It was the first time someone had publicly acknowledged that I was doing better. She spent extra time with me during recesses trying to help me read and do my work. She was the last and only teacher that realized that I had something—that I was worth the effort. Looking back, I appreciate her for doing that. She provided crucial support to a child in need and gave me some relief from the teasing from the other children.

It was also, however, my first realization that I was different.

After that, I never talked about it, and no one else

did either. I got passed along without a word. My fourth-grade teacher was upset with me for "reading" *The Giving Tree* by Shel Silverstein for a book report because he said my reading level should be far past that. The problem was he didn't question it further. Of course, a fourth grader should have been reading something more challenging than *The Giving Tree*. Of course, my reading level should have been higher than that.

It should have been, but it wasn't.

Maybe he assumed that if I had made it to the fourth grade that I was just lazy and picked an easy book for an easy grade. He was a "take no crap" kind of teacher, so it would make sense that he thought this way. He was also a kind man. Fourth grade happened to be the year that my parents got divorced, and I had gained a significant amount of weight as a result. It's possible that he saw I was hurting and wanted to give me a pass, unaware of how that might hurt me further.

Whatever the reason might have been for not digging deeper into the issue, I don't tell this part of the story to cast blame. I do it to point out how easy it can be for a child's struggle to go undiscovered, and how, with enough time, they will do anything to keep it from being revealed. The struggle can be there much earlier than you think, especially because all of the signs might not be there.

Those signs might not be present because your child has figured out how to mask them. I did.

Memorization became a tool for me—one that I developed early on and hadn't fully realized. As a child, we did daily Bible study. Part of that meant reciting quotes from scripture back to the teacher to show that we had learned the material. For example, we had to quote John 3:16. There was no way I could read words like "begotten." However, hearing them spoken over and over again allowed me to remember the word, and though I couldn't sound out the word, I learned at what point in the sentence it was supposed to be.

As I got older, when I had to do a class reading, I would pay attention to the pattern the teacher used to call on students to read. I would count the desks and figure out which paragraph I would be responsible for when my time came up. Counting ahead, I would look for the words I already learned through memorization, from having heard them before and remembering what they looked like.

There were, of course, words I didn't recognize. I

lacked the ability to sound them out, so I would whisper to people close to me, "What is this word? How about this one?" Once I'd gotten the words, I'd practice them, whispering them to myself over and over until I'd memorized them. Once the reading reached me, I was able to fake my way through it.

Until someone messed up the order. Someone always messed up the order. Then I was the kid in the class who needed help with every other word. Those situations were so embarrassing. No one wants to be the kid slurring his words. No one wants to be the cause of other students rolling their eyes when it's their turn to read. No matter how much memorization I achieved, there was always a chance my strategy wouldn't work. I had to adjust and memorize more than one paragraph, and even then, there was no guarantee I had memorized the right one because of someone else's error.

The stress of it was almost unbearable. The best days were when you realized that there weren't enough paragraphs in the day's reading to reach your desk. Then I could just sit back and listen. I would follow along and try to memorize the words that were new to me. I don't even know that I realized I was actually using memorization. I was simply trying to survive in the moment.

I didn't always. Sometimes, I messed up badly. Once, I had miscalculated so badly that I was unable to read a word I had easily "read" the day before. Another time, I read the entirely wrong paragraph.

I wouldn't let that happen again. As part of my calculations, I would learn the words in the paragraphs before and after the one I thought I had to read based on the number of desks in the classroom. I practiced multiple paragraphs and multiple scenarios until I felt confident that my system had no holes. On one occasion, the teacher had to stop me from reading because I had gone into the next paragraph that was meant for the next student behind me.

It is important to note that my strategy had done nothing to improve my actual reading comprehension. I wasn't reading in the strict definition of the word. If I had seen a word previously and heard it said out loud, I was able to memorize it for a certain amount of time. However, if I forgot that word and saw it again later, I could not sound it out. I had to ask for help to memorize it again in the moment.

The truth was even if I would have been able to even attempt to sound it out, I never had the chance. Kids, whether from wanting to help or from impatience, would shout out the words to me when I got stuck on them. Sounding it out wasn't an option because the option was removed. Not wanting to be different or discovered, I took advantage of it. It was also part of my competitive nature. I didn't want to give them the opportunity to yell out those words, so I memorized them first.

In doing so, I felt some sense of accomplishment in having gamed the system, not realizing that I felt accomplished about the wrong thing.

Though you'll learn more about my journey throughout this book, it's also important that you understand that I still don't have the ability to sound out words I don't know. I can't read phonetically. I didn't even learn what that actually meant until only a few short years ago.

What I did learn, as will you, is that you or your loved ones are not alone. Not by a long shot.

AN ILLITERACY EPIDEMIC

I wanted to know more about reading disabilities. What I discovered was mind-blowing.

A friend helped me perform an internet search which revealed to me that more than 32 million Americans can't read. However, upon further research, I discovered that approximately 21 percent of the population—between twenty-one and fourty-four million Americans—are also ranked in the lowest reading levels by grade.

There are more recent studies with more updated numbers, but this is not an academic book about statistics. What is more important is the impact that discovering those numbers had on me. Consider that there is only one state in the US that has a population of more than thirty-two million people. Every other state has less than that. That means that if you took that same thirty-two million from the study and put them in your state, then everyone around you would be unable to read.

Looking at it in that light was sobering. Not only did it allow me to realize that I wasn't alone but that people shared my difficulties at epidemic levels—as bad as any true disease.

In addition, the study excludes Native Americans, at least in a specific sense. When it comes to listing demographics, they are placed in the category "other." As someone who is part Native American, I took special note of this. We are often an omitted class of people. It points to more than one bias in the study. Not only are they excluding groups of people, but in doing so, they ignore access—or a lack thereof—to certain types of schools, to special education teachers trained to recognize these struggles. To libraries or bookstores.

It led me to wonder: how many "others" are suffering that aren't accounted for?

The takeaway here is that the number of individuals struggling with reading is staggering. It is greater than the number of people who reside in my home state of Washington. Imagine everyone around you being unable to read. Imagine them going through what I went through, looking for ways to hide their disability, driven to hide it from fear, anxiety, and embarrassment.

So many people are suffering in silence. As overwhelming as the number is in the study, I can guarantee that in reality—even with updated statistics from more recent studies—the actual number is much, much larger.

AN ODD COMFORT

While these numbers are frightening, you or your child or loved one might be able to find an odd comfort in the statistics.

You are not alone.

The pain and fear and humiliation you've felt, either in public or in private? Someone else has, too. In fact, a lot of people have. That doesn't mean that your feelings are any less important. They are yours and they are real.

My hope is that as we continue together on this journey through this book, you will help someone close to you find the strength to embrace those feelings. Doing so allows them the space to conquer them, as well as any other obstacles that get in their path along the way. Understanding that this will be a struggle, that there will be hard times, and that there will be times when they want to quit will make it that much easier for them *not* to. Knowing that others like myself have experienced the same gives truth to the idea that there is strength in numbers.

As a parent, friend, or relative, you must create an environment where they can share these feelings with you, even if it's hard for you to understand them. Sometimes, it will be hard to understand, particularly if you've never struggled with reading. Still, you must tell them that it's okay to be upset or frustrated.

Equally, if not more importantly, help them reframe their challenges into something positive. It sounds strange, but it can be done.

I turned my disability into a superpower. I'll tell you how they—and you—can, too.

Chapter Two

WHAT'S YOUR SUPERPOWER?

When I got to junior high school, there was no more public reading—no more counting desks. During recess breaks or in the hallway in between classes, I would go up to other students and get their take on whatever book we were supposed to read. The sales pitch often went, "Hey, I didn't have time to read the book. Tell me what it was about." Depending on the assignment, sometimes I'd ask them for their opinion on the chapter, and I'd nod my head, telling them that's what I thought, too.

Then in class, I would raise my hand and give my two cents about the book's content, once I was confident I had a grasp on what the chapters were about. I always found a way to participate in the group discussions about the book—*The Outsiders*, *The Adventures of Tom Sawyer,* and *Animal Farm*—you name it. My teachers, at least to my knowledge, never had a clue.

When you have to read as a child, when you get through a book and have no idea what it actually said, it is beyond frustrating. Almost none of the words made any sense. I've lost count of the times I sat alone, crying, wishing that touching the page would let the information be absorbed into me, or wishing that I had the power to speed-read.

That wasn't real life. Real life meant developing strategies and learning through trial and error. How do you do that without being overwhelmed with anger, feeling that things just aren't fair?

You reframe your struggles, or, more importantly, you reframe the strategies you use to overcome them. When I describe how I asked other students about the books, along with the ability I developed to count the desks that I spoke about in the previous chapter, people came back with, "Well, that's cheating. That's weak."

Wrong. None of those are examples of cheating. Those are examples of how I never gave up and kept moving forward—something I still do today.

Those are examples of my superpowers.

STRENGTH COMES FROM WEAKNESS

Almost every comic book is about a normal person who is given some great power. Most times, they weren't born with it. It meant that almost anyone could become a superhero. Almost. What made them truly great was that they already had a defined character. They already had heroic traits—their superpowers just allowed them to do more with their heroism.

Captain America was a puny soldier before he took the super serum, but he had more heart and bravery than men twice his size. Peter Parker was a whiz kid who wanted to do the right things before he was bitten by a radioactive spider. Matt Murdoch was a blind attorney, fighting for justice in the courts before an accident made him Daredevil.

They took those perceived weaknesses—small stature, nerdiness, blindness—and turned them into strengths. They made their powers even greater because they took the things that made them supposedly weak and used them together with their new abilities.

In junior high, asking those other students, I learned to listen before I spoke. In doing so, I essentially absorbed their abilities. They read and understood the material. I couldn't do that, but I could ask question after question until I did, and I did it in a way that didn't reveal my "secret identity."

At first, I felt like Rogue from the X-Men, but I remembered that she only absorbed people's powers for a little while, and it left them drained. I realized that I was more like Peter Petrelli, from the television show, "Heroes." I was able to take in all of their powers of comprehension and make them my own.

I utilize this skill even today as an adult. I make a point of asking questions. No longer is there any fear of looking like I don't know something. If someone knows more than me about a particular topic? Great! I'm going to ask and ask and ask until I feel like I understand it almost as well as they do. Asking questions is a priceless skill in business, but so many people are afraid to ask them because they feel like it makes them look uneducated.

I realize that these seem like simple ideas—that there's nothing special or "super" about this ability. Ask yourself honestly how often you've gone into a conversation with someone without bringing your own bias. How many times have you not heard what that person had to say because you were thinking about what you were going to say next? Listening with empathy is a skill and one that needs to be developed, especially when a reading disability is involved. Speaking from personal experience, there is a natural defensiveness that must be set aside in order to access your listening superpower.

A favorite mentor once told me: "You have two ears and one mouth for a reason. Listen twice as often as you speak."

In addition to my ability to listen with empathy, counting the desks was a development of my superpower of predictive ability. Like Dr. Strange using the time gem to see different futures, I would figure out when it was my time to read and memorize every word I could so no one would know. This converted to another valuable skill for me in other aspects of my life. In business, it's important to be able to "see around corners"—to predict problems before they happen in order to keep things running smoothly.

When speaking with your child or loved one about their challenge or reading disability, help them see it as a means of amplifying another ability they might have. Doing so will allow them to then use those skills to build the reps it takes to improve their reading ability.

The truth is, there are no radioactive spiders who will help them fix their inability to read overnight. Reframing, however, is a powerful tool to help them along their journey.

THE MUFFIN TEST

I often ask parents: Would you give your kids cake for breakfast?

The answer to this question, as you can imagine, is almost always no.

Let's consider this idea: Imagine you work for a company that sells and markets cake products. You decide you're missing out on more sales because it's only been marketed as something people eat for dessert, or on special occasions. How can you get adults and parents to buy into the idea of eating cake for breakfast, capturing a whole new market and increasing your sales?

You call it a muffin.

No one thinks twice about having a muffin for breakfast. If you are eating a muffin for breakfast, know that you are really eating cake by another name. It's all about a mindset shift. The truth is, you probably realize that you're eating cake, but you've gotten your mind around the idea by buying into the muffin marketing.

In the same way, I want you and those close to you to reframe the thinking around reading struggles, reading disabilities, and disadvantages. Realize that we're going to call them something different.

We're going to say, "What advantage can I find from this challenge? What superpower can I develop because of this? What can I become because of this?"

As a parent, if you realize that your child is using a strategy to get around their reading disability, don't discourage them or tell them they need to stop. Embrace it. Acknowledge it and let them grow from a strength they developed to outsmart a problem in a way that is beyond what is expected from them. Through that, they will develop their unique superpower, which brings them one step closer to overcoming their reading challenge.

If your child asks for a muffin when you tell them they can't have cake for breakfast? Don't deny them. Give them that muffin as a reward for developing a different way to look at a cake.

AVOID BLAME

I came from a working-class family. My parents worked hard and struggled financially. Still, they wanted better for me than what I got from the public school system at the time, largely due to a fear of gang violence in the school, which was a very real problem at the time. They put me in a private Christian school with the thought that I would get the best education there. Looking back though, I wonder now if a public school might have had better resources to figure out my problem. They often had identifiers they could use and were able to accommodate special needs.

If you're a parent, and you're paying extra money for your child to go to a private school, why wouldn't you think they would have these same resources? It was no fault of their own. My mother is a good reader, and she would read to me at a younger age. I was able to retain what she read to me. Because of that, when I later had to do book reports, I'd procrastinate until the very last minute, then ask her to read to me so that I could get through the assignment faster and turn it in on time.

It's possible that your child or loved one has been successful in keeping this from you for longer than you care to admit. If so, you must realize that it's not your fault. When someone can't read, they internalize so much—not just the fact that they can't, but all of the emotions connected with it.

I never blamed my parents for not knowing. I don't blame my teachers for not figuring it out. Don't blame yourself, either.

If you're reading this book, you probably already suspect that someone in your life has these challenges. Use these examples of strategies that I developed as possible warning signs that someone you know might be struggling. Utilize the superpower discussion to approach them and to acknowledge their challenges as a first step towards helping them through it.

If you're listening to this on an audiobook—if you yourself struggle with reading—do not get caught up in the blame game. Do not blame your teachers and parents for not recognizing your struggle. Chances are, you've gotten so good at working around it with your superpower that it would be extremely difficult for them to figure it out. That's nothing to be ashamed of. Don't blame yourself, either. You're working muscles in your brain to get you to a better place.

Remember, just like the heroes in the comics, your superpower is that you're different from others in that you have a unique ability to turn a negative situation into a positive. You can adapt and grow to become a better person *because* the odds are against you—not in spite of them being so. The strategies you have—and will—develop do not make you weaker. They make you stronger.

When you come to accept this, you might feel like you now want to reveal these challenges that either you or your loved one faces to those close to you. It's not a wrong or bad instinct. At the same time, if you're someone reading this in order to help someone in your life, you might want to encourage that person to reveal it to you, and to others, in order for them to have as much help as possible.

However, I want to share with you the story of when I did so and offer some insight about what can happen with this kind of revelation.

Chapter Three

THE SECRET REVEALED

Would you read a book to get a job?

If I think about my younger self and what his answer would be, I'd have to lean towards no. Still, the idea intrigued me, so I decided to see what it would look like to test my hypothesis in real life.

One of the businesses I owned was a small chain of convenience stores. I was starting to hear complaints from customers about some of the younger people working there. There seemed to be a general lack of work ethic and poor customer service. I decided I needed to nip this in the bud.

Using audiobooks, I read through many customer service and human resources books because I wanted to find an answer to the problem. One solution I came up with was to start a book club at the company. I wanted to discuss the books with anyone else who was willing to listen to me. I also saw it as a good way to bring the company together. A decent amount of people participated, and it was fun. I decided to have us read *The Customer Rules: The 39 Essential Rules for Delivering Sensational Service,* by Lee Cockerell, and then talk about it in terms of how we could improve our customer service. We read it over a month and then met to give our thoughts. The discussions were excellent, and our company demonstrated a positive turnaround in our customer service.

Those results sparked an idea.

I'd been left with a stack of five copies of the book, and it just so happened one day I had five interviews. I had to figure out how I was going to get those five applicants down to one as we only had the single position available, so during the interview process, I handed the book out to those applicants. If people wanted to work for me, they were going to have to work harder to get the job in the first place. Giving out the book to applicants was an expensive venture for sure, but it would be worth it as a means to create a buffer for those who didn't want to put in the effort. If they weren't willing to read to get the job, it was a pretty sure sign to me that they wouldn't have the level of work ethic to keep customers from complaining.

The funny thing is: it worked.

Of the five applicants, only one read it and was able to prove that she had done so. It worked out for the best because she turned out to be a stellar employee. The idea had proven to be an effective filter, so I started doing it with everyone who applied for a job.

This inspired me to also keep the book club going within the company, but a funny thing happened. People stopped signing up.

It was the year prior that I had discovered the wonder that is Audible. I had been listening to audiobooks like a madman. I found out there was an option to listen to the books at a higher speed and began consuming them at an even greater rate. The result was that I talked about books endlessly at work, pushed them on all of my employees, and told them they had to read this, that, and the other.

If someone came to me with a problem? Hey, read this book. I had an idea to implement for the business? Guys, guess what, I got it from this book.

About a year after implementing the interview standard, a year of talking up books whenever I got the opportunity, an employee pulled me aside and said, "Will, we're not you. We can't read as much as you do."

It made me realize that I had to explain this new passion—why I was like a kid in the candy store with all of these books. Only three people in my life up until that point had known. How could I find the courage to actually reveal this to the people who worked for me?

Someone else found it for me.

One of my employees came to me and told me he was dyslexic. His numbers were backwards, and his words were all jumbled up. He was afraid of losing his job. Immediately, I told him my secret, without even thinking. I told him I would never put him in a situation where he would be headed for failure and set him up with a different job. Telling him without carefully considering it first gave me the confidence to do what I knew I needed to do.

I needed to tell my story.

We had a large company training, one where all of the employees were there. I sat down and told them all why books meant so much to me—why I wanted to use books to help them in whatever ways they needed.

"I can't read," I told them.

I explained that I could not sound out words. That I was the kid in school everyone yelled the words out to when we had to read out loud in class. That I faked it for years and found ways around revealing it to anyone.

It was an emotional moment but one I hoped would inspire them.

UNEXPECTED RESULTS

Several people came up to me afterwards to tell me they had a spouse or loved one who struggled with reading.

I had it in my mind that revealing my struggle would somehow unite the team—that they would find some motivation from the idea that, *hey, Will did this. There should be nothing we can't do. We understand his obsession with books and why they are important. That struggles can be overcome and that there is a payoff to working hard.*

That didn't happen. It confused me for a while. How could people not connect with this? Here I'd had all these successes, opened all of these businesses despite not being able to read. Why wouldn't my story move them in the way I thought it would?

It occurred to me that, for the most part, people don't care about your struggle unless they can in some way identify with it. It would be nice to believe in the idea that everyone wants to do good for others and help someone besides themselves, but I've learned in this journey, and in particular from this reveal, that self-interest plays a big part in how helpful or encouraging people want to be.

If someone isn't experiencing an equal struggle, how are they going to be inspired? How will they think anything more than, "Hey, that was a cool story?" They can't connect because if someone can read and has always been able to, they can't put themselves in your shoes.

It is for this reason that I caution you—whether the

parent or friend or partner of someone who struggles, or as someone listening to this who cannot read—do not share your struggle with everyone. Nothing magical happens when you do so without carefully choosing your audience. In fact, you might open yourself to harm. Take the time to consider the people in your life and how you think they might actually react, not how you'd want or hope for them to.

It's true that if you share the secret of your child or loved one's struggle, or if you share it yourself that you might encounter others who share the struggle. I don't mean to say that that's impossible. However, if you go into this with the assumption that you'll receive a bunch of universal love and support, you are setting yourself up for disappointment, which is the last thing you need at such a crucial point in the journey.

Ask yourself what your motivation is to share your struggle. Is it to get help? Is it to get sympathy? Is it to stop hiding? These are all questions you have to answer before making what can be a truly huge decision.

If I had to do it over again? Honestly, I'm not sure. In one way, telling the truth lifted this enormous weight. I felt lighter. It inspired me to move forward to research just how bad this problem was and opened dialogues for me that I would have never had before.

On the other hand, part of me says I would not do it again because of the disappointment I mentioned above. I didn't get this glorious swell of support from everyone around me. In many ways, I was still on my own.

I now use my truth as a tool to navigate conversations as a leader because I can say with confidence: Here is my struggle. Here is what I have accomplished. You have no excuses.

If you can, make your revelation a tool that works for you. If you're a parent, use it to find others who may offer some type of support group. Find other parents who have come up with strategies you might not have considered. If you yourself struggle, use your reveal to give you the confidence to move forward and find ways to get the help you need. It's an important first step if you choose to take it.

When you read or can encourage others to read with a purpose, you spark a desire in yourself and in others to read more. In the next chapter, we'll talk about just how to do that.

Chapter Four

READ WITH A PURPOSE

Don't just read. Apply what you read so you can learn.

A few years ago, like most young kids, my thirteen-year-old daughter wanted the newest iPhone.

I'm a firm believer in never taking from a child their wants and needs. You want them to know what it is to want something, to feel as though they need things.

Giving them what they want without working for it? That's another thing altogether.

It was a struggle for me to get to where I am today, to have this level of success, and because it was hard, I appreciate it all the more. In my relationships, with the people I work with, and especially my children, I put struggles in front of them. Challenges to accept. Only then can you truly appreciate whatever it was you wanted.

When my daughter asked for the new phone, without hesitation, I gave her a task. Read *Why Didn't They Teach Me This in School? 99 Personal Money Management Principles to Live By,* by Cary Siegel. She immediately agreed, took the book to her bedroom, and read. Twenty minutes or so went by, and she came out of her room.

"Dad, can I do this with Audible?"

At this time, she knew about my reading difficulties, and my love affair with audiobooks. I, of course, said yes. She downloaded the app and was off. Being that she was a teenager, I knew, just knew that she'd put this task off. A week, maybe two. A month, more likely.

The next day, I picked her up from her mother's house. As she got in the car, she told me she had about twenty minutes left in the book and wanted to go get the new iPhone today.

I couldn't believe it. She'd almost finished the book in less than one night, using my own method against me. Still somewhat doubtful, I quizzed her. To my surprise, we talked about the book the entire car ride. She hadn't just done a speed read, not paying attention. She took in the information and understood it, well enough to have a conversation with her father about it.

We talked about money lessons, things about managing finances that took me a lifetime to learn, through just as many failures as successes. I shared with her my fear of children being taken advantage of financially, and how I wanted her to read this book, so she was equipped with the knowledge to prevent that as she grew older—to learn from my mistakes so she never found herself playing catch-up with her money. Given a goal, she read with a purpose. I couldn't have been prouder.

I wanted to show her more.

I reached out to the author to see if he would come speak to our tribal youth at a financial camp they organize every year. He agreed, and they put on a special event just for the kids. He gave a fantastic talk, giving the kids a lot of useful information.

Best of all, my daughter got to meet him. He signed

her hard copy of the book, which excited her to no end. She hugged me, and I whispered in her ear, "I did this all for you."

I wanted to show her the results of her effort, to give meaning to reading, to see that the results went far beyond what she might have imagined. She has become an avid reader, using Audible frequently when she has big assignments for school. We have conversations about the books she's reading.

FIND THEIR "WHY"

Reading with a purpose inspired in her a desire to read. She was given a goal and a path, and in following that path and achieving that goal, she unlocked a love for reading. If your child or loved one has challenges reading, and therefore can't find the motivation to try, you must help them find their "why."

I'd been training in martial arts for a couple of years as sort of a bucket list challenge for myself. The place where I chose to train, while not terribly far away, had horrible traffic during the time of my commute. It was a solid hour there and a solid hour home. This time really fed into my Audible obsession, as I would consume books—mostly about business—on the rides there and back.

My training was moving along nicely until I was derailed by a shoulder injury. There was a large tear, and it prevented me not only from participating in martial arts but in any kind of exercise at all. I've always struggled with my weight, and the martial arts were not only helping me keep it in check but lose it. That all stopped with the injury. The weight came back quickly, and it felt like there was nothing I could do.

Then a thought occurred to me.

"You're this self-proclaimed reading guru," I told myself. "So read a diet book."

I found *The Bullet Proof Diet,* by Dave Asprey. I listened to it at any available opportunity, from the flight to a vacation destination to the flight back and any free time in between. I followed every detail, and within two months, I had lost almost forty pounds. My injury helped me to find a new "why."

If your children or loved ones are struggling, or if they are avoiding reading, you must help them reframe reading as a method to solving their problems. This is crucial in helping them find a purpose to their reading, or in working to learn how to read.

Equally as critical is helping them understand that

every grief, every loss, and every perspective on those things—someone has written about it.

Whatever struggle you or your child may be experiencing? Someone, somewhere, has written about it. The weight gain I experienced—someone wrote about it. The challenges you're having reading, or hiding the fact that you or your child can't read?

I wrote about it.

Motivation is a funny thing. It tends to be different for everyone, particularly in school. The child who isn't paying attention isn't necessarily unintelligent. Perhaps they are daydreaming about something grand—some larger accomplishment. Progressing through the grade system and earning high marks doesn't drive everyone the same way. It did nothing for me. All I could ever think of in school was what was beyond it for me—what I would do for a living once I was done—of owning my own business, whatever it might be. Of course, my teachers would tell me that in order to get a good job, I'd have to get good grades. However, even if the job is their motivation, the grades won't resonate with them and it won't motivate them to read. Without dreamers, we wouldn't have the joy of places like Disneyland.

Find out what your child's interests are, not just now, but for the future, and find them a book about that topic. Be interested in the books with them. Ask your child about the books, not to see if they've read them—although that helps—but to let them see that you are engaged and invested in their improvement. Your interest will increase theirs.

NONFICTION IS IMPORTANT

I'll say it: I'm not a fan of fiction.

I was never a fan of it growing up and I'm not one now. It might be a shortsighted view, but I believe nonfiction holds more importance because it documents real life—something that actually happened. It's helped me and countless others understand the world we live in.

This isn't to say that fiction cannot teach life lessons. It absolutely can. I would never discourage anyone from reading *anything*. For younger kids, however, I strongly feel that nonfiction is what you should be encouraging your children to read because there is inspiration to be found in the true-life stories of others.

If your child is into video games or computers, find

them a book about the founder of Nintendo or Steve Jobs. Let them learn about their struggles, as well as their successes. If they want to be a professional athlete, no matter how difficult that might be, give them a book about a player who made it against all the odds because their stories may be more similar than you realize.

My dad always told me that anyone could be president if they worked hard enough. I believed it so deeply that it led me to do something that would set the course for the rest of my life. I always noticed that presidents read their speeches using teleprompters. Imagine the fear in my mind that came with realizing that fact. I was afraid to read in class—how would I do it in front of the nation as president? Still, my father made me feel like it was an absolute possibility. I knew, though, that I would never be able to rely on notes for public speaking. I'm so glad that he gave me the encouragement to be president because it inspired me to practice, practice, practice. It is why I am the public speaker I am today.

Now I don't know that I would have been a great politician, but the point is that we always want to inspire our kids to be the best that they can be—to succeed even greater than their imagination. When you have an opportunity, put that inspiration in front of them in the form of a book about someone who achieved in that same way.

Without shared knowledge—from both past and current generations—we would not be where we are today. The sharing of that knowledge began with books.

It's important to remember, too, that there was a time when the average person wasn't allowed access to that knowledge—that keeping them from that information, or any information, was a way of keeping them separate and unequal from other parts of society.

We've discussed earlier that literacy levels aren't well documented or well represented when it comes to Native people, other people of color, and those of a lower socioeconomic status. Now that we have access to books in ways we never had before—cheap, affordable methods like libraries—we have a responsibility to not only encourage our children and those who struggle as adults to read but to read about their history and their culture through the eyes of someone who lived it. We must encourage them to read—with the use of audiobooks in particular—for the past generations who suffered these same inequalities so that they might do what their ancestors would have never dreamed possible for themselves or those that came after.

EASIER THAN EVER

Once you've made up your mind to help your child, or to help yourself, the good news is there are more tools now than ever before to help you overcome your obstacles. In the next chapter, I'll share with you the many technologies that I used in the hopes that they can make your journey just a little bit easier.

Chapter Five

TECHNOLOGY IS KEY

I tried going back to college after I had a family—a wife and two daughters. Going back is hard to begin with, let alone with others to take care of. Still, the fact that I hadn't finished my degree seemed to be a hang-up for the people around me, and it made me feel self-conscious. I wanted to inspire my daughters to achieve.

One class per quarter was all I had time for as, by this point, I was already running multiple businesses. I took a laptop to class because I typed very quickly, and the easiest way for me to understand the material was to take notes in that way.

Yes, I said "typed." Stay tuned—I'll explain.

This was my method for each class. The only way for me to retain all of the information was to essentially take dictation and type out everything the professors said. It worked out great until I ran into a problem. One of the professors on the first day of class stated that there was no technology allowed in the classroom—no laptops, no cell phones. Nothing.

It made no sense to me. We were grown adults. What did it matter what we used to learn the material as long as we learned it? Who was he to make that rule and keep people from doing whatever it took to collect his notes from class?

I had been warned about taking his class before signing up. A number of students didn't like him and said that he wasn't the most caring or understanding professor. Still, I wanted to give it a shot. Not too long after the semester began, my children's grandmother passed away. I left my professor a message to let him know I wouldn't be in class that week, but I never received a response.

Going back to school was already difficult enough. I didn't want to be there in the first place and felt like I was there out of obligation. Not being able to use my laptop, coupled with a professor who couldn't be bothered was the final straw. My businesses were important and needed my focus, so I dropped out for the final time. There are stories of wildly successful individuals who didn't finish school. In my time, it was Bill Gates and the other dot-com millionaires of that era. Today, it's people like Mark Zuckerberg. They didn't finish and look what they accomplished. That's what I told myself. However, I also knew—as you should now—that if you're not going to college, you need to plan to be a reader for the rest of your life.

I never found out why the professor didn't allow technology in the classroom, but I think to him it represented a distraction. He didn't give a thought to the people who might be struggling that used that technology to assist them.

GET OVER IT

In my journey, I've found that lack of empathy with the use of technology all too common. There are far too many preconceived notions about the influence of technology, especially in the lives of children and younger adults. People constantly talk about the negative aspects of social media, and how we don't know how to relate to each other anymore. They complain that technology is ruining their children. When I shared with someone the story of how I gave my daughter an iPhone after reading a book, I was greeted with what I can only call snark.

Technology is not ruining your kids. In fact, you are doing them a disservice if you think the gadgets they have at their disposal today are harmful. You have to ask them the right questions about how they're using that technology to determine if they're using it in ways that can be helpful to them.

My daughter used technology to "outsmart" me to earn her iPhone. I didn't punish her for using Audible instead of reading the physical copy of the book. I praised and rewarded her because she found a way to make technology work for her. Not only that, but her reward gave her access to the types of programs and applications that can further her journey into reading.

Parents: Get over yourself. Come to grips with the fact that the technology is here and it's not going anywhere. Better still, get comfortable with it. Believe me, I understand that for many of us, this is not the world we grew up in. We came up with the idea that you had to do much more to access knowledge and information, to get a job, or to learn a skill.

If we don't embrace the changes of our current time, we will be left behind. You might be okay with that but consider that it might also leave behind your children. How they utilize the vast amount of technology at their fingertips has so much to do with your outlook. Consider having your children listen to audiobooks as part of their "digital activities." Ensure that they are involving some form of reading anytime they're engaging in screen time.

If I had some of the tools available today, I know that I would not have struggled as I did.

Teachers now embrace it. My daughter told me they now allow smartphones in her classroom. She's actually called me from class. Of course, I don't encourage her to use her phone inappropriately in class, and neither do her teachers. If their work is done, they aren't sticklers about how they use them, as long as they aren't a disruption to the rest of the class. They create an environment where the smartphone isn't some evil device.

While it's true most of the list that follows can be found on a phone, I recognize that not everyone has the access—financially or otherwise—to modern smartphones. The wonderful thing about most libraries today is they are filled with computers, and they're free to use. This might seem like a fairly obvious statement, but it's easy to forget the number of free and affordable services that are part of the library system. They also offer free audiobooks. Remember—I will continue to remind you that listening to books is reading.

YouTube: What *can't* you find on YouTube nowadays? From putting together a piece of furniture to makeup tutorials, there is a wealth of knowledge on the site. Did you know, though, that you can find books there? I once had an employee inform me that a book I assigned to her was available for free on YouTube and she listened to it for free there. An excellent feature with YouTube is that you can speed up the video to watch at whatever is a comfortable pace for you.

Dictation software: What I love about dictation software is it allows you to pronounce words correctly. If it doesn't understand what you're saying, it won't recreate the word. If your child can pronounce a word, the software will spell it out and they can see how the word is supposed to look. This is invaluable, particularly for dyslexics who see the letters in an incorrect order.

Google: When I was memorizing words, I had to

ask kids in school to tell me what words were that I didn't recognize. If you're using a dictation software that doesn't have the ability to read something back to you, or if you're using your computer's microphone, you can speak the word into a Google search. Google then has an option when they return with the definition of the word to hear how that word is pronounced.

Grammarly: This is an add-on available on Google Chrome. It is a terrific help with my emails. Grammarly will edit your whole email by judging whether or not your content is grammatically correct.

Audible: My absolute favorite on this list, and a no-brainer as to why and how this technology is useful. Like YouTube, Audible offers different speeds at which you can listen to the book, allowing you to consume more information in a greater amount of time. Just ask my daughter.

I ALMOST MISSED OUT

I almost never signed up for Audible. I am admittedly cheap, and the service seemed expensive to me. The first two books I listened to were free, but I wasn't willing to spend the $14.95 a month to continue. I doubted I could read even one book per month. Then I considered I was paying just as much for Netflix, and that I couldn't justify that over something that would actually help me with my reading challenges. I signed up for a month, which quickly turned into a year, which led to my current obsession with Audible today.

My point is: don't make my initial mistake. If you're spending money on something that does nothing to help your reading challenges, rethink that priority. Give yourself a chance at a month and see if you don't end up with the same obsession. The wrong priorities might be holding you back from greatness.

PRAISE FOR THE INNOVATORS

I love to research the things that I encounter in everyday life. It fascinates me to no end to learn how things originated, who invented them and why—particularly when it comes to some of the tools I've used to help me with my reading struggles.

What surprised me—though it really shouldn't have—is that the daughter of Audible's founder is dyslexic. He formed it because he wanted to help others like his daughter who shared her struggle. While Amazon bought the company a number of years ago, he continues to run that division. It's an amazing story and one that gives me a great deal of inspiration.

I've always loved the quote from the film *Wall Street II* that "a fisherman always sees another fisherman from afar." A person who struggles with reading can often see it in someone else, and not just in the things they say or do. It's because of this that I think it is more than likely that the options on YouTube, the spoken word function on Google, and tools like Grammarly were designed or inspired by someone who had difficulty reading or had someone in their life who did. They made those tools and advancements in the technology for people like us.

I want to thank all of those people at Apple; all the people who program the dictation software; all the people at these enormous companies who might never know the impact their innovation has had. Without Amazon, without Audible, where would I be? Had they not created these things, I wouldn't be able to share my story with you.

If your children struggle, tell them that the next Audible might be in them. Inspire them and motivate them to embrace technology. As long as it continues to progress and develop, they will have the opportunity to see the world in ways we never did. They'll have opportunities we didn't.

The next innovation might be theirs.

NEGATIVITY *WILL* COME

My grandmother told me a story when I was younger. She had a cousin who was quite smart, and they would write letters back and forth to each other. She told him at one point that she was afraid to write to him because she didn't have his education or his intelligence and didn't want to use the wrong words.

He reassured her by telling her that the sign of a true lack of intelligence was in pointing out the mistakes of others. When you speak poorly of someone else's spelling, grammar, or the like, you're highlighting your own ignorance.

That story stuck with me as a child and followed me into adulthood. Not everyone is like her cousin. There are going to be people who judge you for not only having a disability, but for revealing it.

In the next chapter, we'll talk about how to handle those judgments.

Chapter Six

TURN A NEGATIVE INTO A POSITIVE

Don't go around telling everyone you can't read. You will not get the empathy you expect. I don't want to paint everyone with a negative brush, but at the same time, I want to protect you and your children or loved ones from unnecessary pain. Not everyone will see the struggle as you do. Don't go out there and say, "Hey, I'm dyslexic," or, "Guess what? My child has a reading disability." You'd like to believe that everyone will be comforting and supporting, but the reality is quite different.

Stereotypes continue to circle the label of dyslexia. People often associate it with stupidity rather than seeing it as an actual disability. They also assume it means you just read words backwards. Hell, up until I realized I had it, that's what I thought the definition of it was.

That's right. I have dyslexia.

I didn't discover that's what it was until only recently—within the last few years after (surprise, surprise) listening to an audiobook about it. I had been doing research for this book and had read many books on the topic, one of which was *The Dyslexic Advantage: Unlocking the Hidden Potential of the Dyslexic Brain*. In doing so, I discovered that dyslexics have some common shared traits—advanced spatial awareness, for one. They also have the ability to listen to audiobooks at higher speeds than "normal." What was even more interesting was realizing that there are also common misconceptions about what it means to be dyslexic, with most people believing that those with the challenge only see letters backwards. Another difficulty for dyslexics is phonetic spelling—which is my specific issue. I cannot sound out a word by looking at it and so must use one of my many workarounds to determine just what that word is.

When I first thought about writing this book, I

reached out to a local literacy group to organize a time when I could sit down and tell my story to anyone who might be interested. When I arrived, I found it was run solely by volunteers, an older, academic crowd. It reminded me of being in school again. The people who attended the group were also largely of this demographic. When I spoke with one of the volunteers, she told me that there were more people waiting to be paired up than there were of them. I explained to her a brief version of my own story and the workarounds I had created.

She told me it sounded like I was dyslexic.

Getting that confirmation, knowing that I had a real difficulty that could be identified, somehow gave me hope. It inspired me to share my struggles because I could give it a name, one people knew and understood and would therefore—I thought—empathize with my challenges.

As I mentioned, while I earned my associate's degree, I dropped out before earning my bachelor's. In my twenties, people would often tell me about past high school friends going on to college and getting a four-year degree. As such, I never felt "book smart" in comparison. I'd often be referred to as "street smart," which at the time felt like a negative statement.

As I got older, I came to realize that, like my grandmother's relative, that was an example of others voicing their own insecurities and projecting them on me. I like to say:

> "Haters hate because they ain't."

Those who belittle the struggle are angry because you are doing something so extraordinary that they can't wrap their mind around it. To them, dyslexic means stupid, so it's impossible that you've managed to achieve all that you have. They can't accept the fact that you're a secret genius who is learning—or has learned—to turn your weakness into a superpower.

The harsh reality is that, for the most part, people don't care about your or your child's struggle. Everyone is only worried about their own. That's why they speak negatively about your success, why they only have negative comments. They are simply too wrapped up in their own lives to truly care about yours.

For example...

A HARD LESSON LEARNED

When I started to tell people about my reading struggles, I felt a weight lifted off my shoulders. In fact, I got so excited about the feeling that I decided I wanted to inspire people, to get them as excited about reading as I was. I figured they'd see this guy, successful in business despite having a reading difficulty and be motivated to read as much as they could.

I had been on the high of revealing my reading challenges to my own company, and I had an opportunity to expand upon my idea about whether or not someone would read a book to get a job. I also wanted to see if someone would read a book to *keep* a job. I took a position to help out a local retail company who had been having some problems with store management. Immediately, I revealed to the company's upper management that I was dyslexic, along with my plan to make everyone read the book in order to keep working there. The employees weren't necessarily bad ones, but I wanted to shake things up—to give everyone the same baseline of customer service that I had successfully implemented in my own companies.

The first meeting with the store-level employees was my introduction to them as well. I told them,

"Here is *The Customer Rules*. You have until the end of the month to read the book, and here is a free access code to Audible if you need it.

The pushback was immediate. Some of them must have wondered to themselves who this crazy person was, coming in out of nowhere, telling them they had to read. Others made snarky comments. One even went so far as to say, "What's someone with dyslexia supposed to do?"

"I *am* dyslexic," I responded. "That's why I offered you Audible. There is *no* excuse."

The great part from the store level was that it worked! The employees had all read the book and had one-on-one meetings with me to discuss it. In fact, no one got fired for not reading the book because they *all* sat down with me to talk about it. Some of them had such great insights that I took notes on our conversations, as I was learning just as much from them. I also discovered that some of them were dealing with learning challenges of their own, which compelled me to help them even more. I recommended more books, and those who read excelled in their positions. The employees even created a book club and held meetings around other books.

For example, *Verbal Judo*—a book that has helped many companies and police departments learn valuable tactics for hostile situations—became the book to read for the security team and the front-line supervisors, as it helped them de-escalate situations with angry customers.

Everything was going great—at the store level.

Despite what I had seen as a success—the employees were doing well in their jobs and were more motivated to come to work—I saw that my enthusiasm wasn't shared at the levels of upper management.

They cut the book budget.

I put together a passionate email making my case for why this was wrong and sent it to everyone in upper management. The response was an accusation that I had not written my own email. The problem was there were people above me at the corporate level who thought, especially because of my telling everyone that I was dyslexic, that I didn't have the intelligence to write an email. They—as is the case with so many people—wrongly tied my challenges to a lack of brainpower.

Worse yet, they accused me of not writing my own

emails. They even went so far as to call out one of my employees and ask them if they wrote it for me.

It's important here to clarify that in spite of my disadvantage I *can* write. It just takes me longer than most. Using the tools we discussed in the previous chapter, I am able to create well-articulated, grammatically correct emails. However, people above me at the corporate level felt I didn't have the intelligence to do so. I wouldn't let this stop me from spreading positivity.

And neither should you.

FIND THE POSITIVES

I realize I'm painting a grim picture about what can happen when you reveal your truth to the world. The email at work took me back to my school days, having the words yelled out to me by my classmates because I was so slow. It took all the momentum I had built by successfully making books part of the job in my other businesses and brought it crashing down. It reminded me of all of my perceived shortcomings that I've dealt with along my journey.

However, let's step forward with a more positive example as to what can happen when you do.

When I was in my late teens to early twenties, I told one of my friends that I struggled with reading. He told me that Richard Branson, the founder of the Virgin brand, was dyslexic. I didn't know I was dyslexic at the time, so even I held some of the stereotypes about the label. Still, I was amazed. My friend said, "And he's a billionaire." It was so inspiring to know that someone had the same challenges and still achieved greatness.

Hearing that inspired me to do something different—to be something different. Ted Turner—billionaire founder of news networks CNN and TBS, to name a few—once said, "Set goals higher than you could ever achieve so you never stop." I put that thought into action by creating my own businesses and creating the life I have for me and my family. Who's to say I would have had that same drive if my friend hadn't told me that—if I hadn't taken a chance on revealing to him my secret?

The negativity will be there, to be sure, but if you choose with whom you share the struggle carefully, great things can come.

If they don't, though? Be better in spite of the negativity. Teach that to your children. The amount of energy put into something someone said, or how they act can be overwhelming and draining. Put that energy into something positive. Don't sit around blaming anyone for your problems. Don't wait for someone to show you how to read or for someone else to help you. Go out and set that goal for yourself—tell yourself you're going to learn to read.

Grind at that goal. Listen to more books. Engage in more reading exercises. Seek help after school. Visualize where you want to be and move towards it. It's not enough to sit back and say you want to read. You have to get up and do it. If your disability has a label like dyslexia, don't use it as a crutch. No woe is me, I have this condition, so I can't do this. No one else is going to do it for you.

Part of dealing with negativity is anger. You're going to get mad. Nothing is better for that anger than a book—specifically books that talk about how to deal with negative perceptions and influences. Two in particular that I recommend for times like those are *The Subtle Art of Not Giving a F*ck,* by Mark Manson, and *You Are a Badass,* by Jen Sincero. The titles alone should give you some idea of how they can help you find inspiration when others place obstacles in your path. They provide you with what I like to call tactical forms of verbal judo that help you navigate negative conversations.

Look past the negative voices. Find a goal that reaches beyond your current situation and go for it. Every time you get angry or frustrated, focus on that vision of who you dream of becoming—then take the steps to make it happen. I firmly believe that if you really want it, you can get it.

Go make a ton of money.

You can. If you're struggling with reading and you are finding similar workarounds and putting in the effort despite your disadvantages, just to do what everyone else does naturally—if you work twenty times harder than everyone else just to pronounce the simplest word? You have what it takes to be rich. You have the grit and determination necessary to make that kind of money. If you can push through all of that and come out on the other side not caring what others think of you, you're going to end up better off than all of those who doubted you.

TRUE GRIT

Your drive will be rewarded.

I saw a need for the city of Tacoma to be viewed in a more positive light. When I was a kid, all you heard about Tacoma were the gangs in the schools, and how parents should never send their kids to them. The city flat out had a bad reputation. There was a local publication there that was failing—too far gone for me to invest in it and save it, so I went another route.

I was going to start a publication of my own.

I posted an advertisement—without proofreading—on Craigslist, looking for writers. A surprising number of people responded, but none seemed quite right for what I had in mind—until I met Sierra Hartman. He was excited and wanted to jump on board right away. I had him perform a series of tasks for my other companies—taking freelance photos and writing articles for me. He had so much enthusiasm that it was a natural fit.

Together, we started gritcitymag.com.

We built a team of terrific freelance writers, writing terrific articles about the brighter side of Tacoma, and it started a grassroots movement. Sierra eventually hired on another person named Sarah Kay, and we all ran the magazine together. Eventually, my other businesses demanded too much of my time, and we negotiated a deal where I would continue funding them until they could survive on their own—which they did. It still exists today.

Sierra later revealed to me why he chose to work with me. It was the grammatically incorrect ad I had placed on Craigslist. So many others had walked away when they saw that, but Sierra told me that he thought to himself, "Should I take a chance on someone who wants to start a magazine but can't write a paragraph?" When he realized I was willing to take a chance on him, he decided to take a chance on me, and he was rewarded with his own company.

Me? My reward is that I get to tell you about the time a man with dyslexia started his own magazine. I get to offer proof that if you want something—differently abled or not—you can make it happen if you're willing to drive towards that goal.

That's real grit. You have it in you. Now use it.

IT TAKES A TEAM APPROACH

What I've described here can sound like it's necessary for you to walk this path alone in order to protect yourself from pain. While it's important to choose your circle carefully, that circle is still absolutely necessary in order for you to make progress in your journey.

You need a team. Let me tell you about the time I truly and fully realized that.

By now you've figured out that there are a number of moments where books changed my life. One of those moments was when I finished listening to Malcolm Gladwell's *Outliers.* I am a fan of all of his books, but this one stuck with me in particular because he talks about how grit and determination lead to unusual success—the way Bill Gates accumulated extreme wealth, the way the Beatles became one of the most successful musical bands of all time. None of them, however, had done it alone.

I was invited to attend a fundraiser at the private school I attended when I was younger. Some speeches were given, and one talked about the journey of someone who had been given funding to attend the school. It was in that moment, fresh off my reading of *Outliers,* that I realized that you cannot get anywhere in life without a team. You cannot achieve great success alone, no matter what form that success takes.

The following year, I asked the principal to allow me back to make a speech of my own—to tell my story. I got the chance to deliver the keynote speech at the next year's fundraiser. I wanted to tell the school donors why I liked the school—why it meant so much to me that offering help to an underprivileged child of low economical means led to him finding success in the world.

My parents struggled to have me attend that school. We were a working-class family. After my parents divorced, my mother couldn't afford to send me there anymore. She put everything on credit cards just to keep us there. Eventually, it became too much. She eventually went to the administrators and told them that she would have to pull us out. They offered her a reduced tuition and a job working in the kitchen, which amounted to us essentially attending for free.

Much of that money came from anonymous donors. It gave me a debt that I wanted to pay back to society. I told the audience of donors about how I now owned multiple businesses. It was through donors like them that I was able to continue at that school and through grit and determination, I was able to forge a successful life for myself. I wanted them to see the real evidence of someone they'd helped.

It also solidified for me the idea that I didn't do any of this alone. Every person in every circumstance in my life led to me being where I am today.

ASSEMBLE YOUR TEAM

Remember that we talked about turning your weakness into your superpower. Most superheroes are part of a team. It's time to bring yours together. If you're waiting for a group to find you, to help you, ask yourself when that has ever happened. You have to seek them out. Sometimes, you'll find them in the most unlikely places. It's been said that we are the sum of the five people we associate with the most—said another way, your net worth is the same as your five closest friends.

You can find team members anywhere. I attended Business Mastery, an event hosted by Tony Robbins. He had just released his book, *Unshakeable*. In the book, Tony discusses his principles for building wealth, as well as the pitfalls associated with financial advisors who aren't working in your best interest. During the event, he talked about the book and, at one point, he brought someone out from his financial firm to talk about his book on stage, and he took questions from the audience. I was looking forward to learning something new. Unfortunately, most of the questions asked had already been answered in his book.

Still, Business Mastery was an exciting event. One aspect of it consisted of those attending being placed in teams of eight people. We were to spend time together during the breaks. During that time,

I overheard two of our team members—one, a man we had nicknamed "The French Guy," and another who owned a chain of gyms in California—sharing frustrations with the questions from the audience. They had both read the book prior to the event, just as I had listened to it on Audible beforehand. I decided to chime in on their conversation. Two other business people in our group had also listened to it on Audible, which was a clue to me that a number of business professionals read books using Audible for the sake of time.

Tony spoke about the concept of proximity at the event—how we should use this gathering as an opportunity to network. As a result, the California gym owner is now my "book buddy." Once a month, we schedule anywhere from a half hour to an hour talking about a book we've chosen to read.

This was a unique circumstance, my finding a "team member" to keep me motivated to read in this way. There are others, to be sure. At the Robbins event, I felt comfortable enough to share my reading struggle, and my team rallied behind my cause. We made T-shirts that said "Leaders 'R' Readers." We put book covers over Tony's book that read: "32 million Americans can't read. If you can read this, you can help."

It was an incredible feeling, realizing there were people who were willing to push my cause forward.

While I warned you about being cautious about sharing your difficulties, don't go to the other end of the spectrum and isolate yourself. You can't take this trip alone. Your struggle has been experienced by others, whether in the past, or currently. Seek out your actual disadvantage and find out how others like you have turned it into their advantage.

Have your child join activities or groups and not necessarily ones that are solely focused on reading and literacy. Get them involved in something that they're passionate about. When you have those feelings of isolation, you have to put yourself out there. If you're in a group of people that share that passion, you might find others who also share your challenges, and you can begin to form your team.

A team standing with you makes it okay. They allow you to do what I call "failing forward." They will be there to support you when you fail, and you will. Failures will occur on this journey, but as with anything else in life, you will learn from those failures, and it is easier to do that when you have the support of others around who either understand or share your struggles.

They will share their mistakes as well. The truth is, you can't live long enough to make all the mistakes you need to in order to improve. You can take power and learn lessons not only from your own "failures," but from those of others.

THERE IS LIGHT

It's a lot of work, all of this. I know. I promise you, though, that the proverbial light at the end of the tunnel is there if you put in the work.

In the next chapter, we'll talk about what it's like on the other side.

Chapter Seven

ON THE OTHER SIDE

When I've told my story to those who can read, they can't comprehend it. They simply don't understand it. Sometimes, they're amazed. Sometimes, they don't actually believe it.

This chapter is for those of you who can't read at all and are listening to this; for those of you who can read but struggle; or for the parents, friends, and relatives of someone who faces these challenges on a daily basis, who know just how real this fight really is because in one way or another, you are living it.

Looking at a word and not knowing what it is can

be one of the most frustrating, gut-wrenching feelings you will ever have, particularly if you're trying to understand that word in a social setting. I recall so many nights, crying alone in my room at night, unable to read in school but too afraid to tell anyone.

All you do in those moments is wish—wish that just by touching the words on the page that you'll magically understand them. Wish that you could know everything in the book without having to put in the work. It only takes so long before you realize that the wishing gets you nowhere. At some point, you have to face your challenge if you want to overcome it.

That's what I did. As I said in the previous chapters, I talked about how, at first, I developed workarounds. Asking the other kids in school what they thought about something we were assigned to read. Memorizing words and counting desks. This was all before I discovered audiobooks.

Yet with all of that, I still struggled. It seemed that though I had come up with these ways to manage my difficulties, I still couldn't read. It was always going to be more work for me than it was for others, and as a result, it felt like there was no light at the end of the tunnel, a feeling I'm sure you as the parent or friend of someone who experiences this can identify with.

There was a point, however, when the light turned on. I can't promise it will happen for everyone, but if telling you what happened for me inspires you to continue on this journey, if it keeps you or your child or loved one from throwing in the towel, then it is a story worth telling.

Somewhere in the middle of using all of these strategies, I learned how to read—but I first had to find the inspiration to change my mindset. I needed something to give me the hope to push through my self-doubt.

The inspiration came from my first "oh my God" moment in my mid to early twenties. Some of you might remember a chain email that went around in the early 2000s called the Cambridge study. It had a paragraph written where the first and last letter of each word was in the right order, but the letters in-between were all mixed up:

> Aoccdrnig to rscheearch at Cmabrigde uinervtisy, it deosn't mttaer waht oredr the ltteers in a wrod are, the olny iprmoetnt tihng is taht the frist and

> lsat ltteres are in the rghit pclae. The rset can be a tatol mses and you can sitll raed it wouthit a porbelm. Tihs is bcuseae we do not raed ervey lteter by it slef but the wrod as a wlohe.

I've inserted the actual jumbled letters from the study in the physical book, but here is what it says:

> According to research at Cambridge University, it doesn't matter what order the letters in a word are, the only important thing is that the first and last letters are in the right place. The rest can be a total mess and you can still read it without a problem. This is because we do not read every letter by itself, but the word as a whole.

Since the time that it first made the rounds on the internet, and in doing my research for this book, I discovered that the whole thing was fake—it's not an actual study. Being able to read it has nothing to do with your level of intelligence. None of that mattered to me, though.

I was able to read it! And this was years before I learned about Audible.

Encouraged by this, I started picking up physical books again. I put in the time to look up words using the technology we discussed earlier. I began memorizing words again—and it worked.

I started slowly reading books again on business and leadership, though I have to admit, it took me quite a while. I had to find time on planes or some other quiet area as it took a lot of focus and I was easily distracted. It took far more energy to concentrate on reading than to go to Google in order to hear words sounded out that I couldn't pronounce. The difference now was that I had the confidence, and I knew that all that extra work would pay off. I was no longer just trying to survive—I finally had my inspiration to thrive.

One of the business books that I physically read was *The Personal MBA* by Josh Kaufman.

When it comes to my accomplishments in business, people often ask me where I went to school to learn the ins and outs. They don't realize that while earning credits towards my bachelor's degree that I dropped out of college—that the school system was terrible for me. The best way for me to learn was with hands-on experience and reading a book.

The Personal MBA talked about how so many waste hundreds of thousands of dollars on business degrees—about how you can pick up every business lesson there is to know if you find the right books and just read, read, read. In fact, at the end of the book, Kaufman gives his list of recommended reads. You can imagine what I did with that list.

Realizing that I could read the physical book opened up new worlds for me. In many ways, I no longer identified with the fact that I couldn't read. Since I enjoyed running businesses, I thought back to earlier in my life—about how I would only look at the comics in the Sunday newspaper, not knowing what the words in the bubbles said. However, I realized later in life I was also doing something else.

I was reading the business briefs, too.

How? By asking questions. I would never do it with the comics because I made up stories in my head based on the pictures. When I read the comics, I would gloss over words I didn't understand, but when I looked at the business briefs, I'd ask my father what certain words meant. I wanted to know what they were and understand their meaning. It was my first sign that business was what I was meant to do. I was encouraged to continue to do so from a lot of positive affirmation from family that I would be good at business. They planted seeds of confidence in me.

All the years of looking up words and figuring out the meaning behind them had paid off. Up until I had seen the Cambridge study, I avoided reading topics that didn't interest me. I didn't realize I was working toward something grander. I was trying to fake it in public readings in school. It was a lot of work to read physical books. I pushed and pushed, and because of that, I was able to take some of those lessons and apply them to my own businesses.

Even as powerful as this realization was, an even more significant event in my life provided me with the ultimate motivation to learn to read.

FROM TRAGEDY COMES TRIUMPH

The day my ex-wife told me she was done with our marriage was, as you can imagine, not a good day. I was overweight, my marriage was crumbling, and my overall stress was at an all-time high. I believe in a higher power—a creator that made us. I hadn't been to church since my school days, but I prayed the prayer of my life. I asked for God, Jesus, the creator in Heaven, whatever that meant, to take my hand, take my life, and do with it as you will because I'm done. I give up. I was truly depressed and saw no hope.

About twenty minutes after learning that my ex-wife

was leaving me, I got the call that my father was killed in a motorcycle accident.

I hit the ground. I punched the door and the walls. I asked God, "What kind of an answer to a prayer is that?"

The combination of those events put me into a dark place. I had lost so much in the space of one day. I know now, though, that there was a purpose. Those things put me in the place to do the things I was destined to do.

At my father's funeral, there were a number of people who told me all the things he had done for them. He was always that guy in the background, but he would just get things done—take on the bureaucracy for other people. I never got to tell my father about my reading disability, but hearing all of those things about him made me decide to do something about it—along with everything else in my life. I began my bucket list that inspired me to travel more and see the world. I began training in martial arts. I discovered Audible out of that boredom during my hour-long commute to martial arts training. I was training both my body and brain to become something different. Listening to audiobooks allowed me to learn from others' perspectives and take on an entirely new outlook on life.

We only have one life, and it can be taken away in an instant.

Like Kaufman said in *The Personal MBA*, all you have to do to learn something is to read, read, read. I did, and the books I consumed helped me become the change I wanted to see in the world. I lost weight. I opened a health food store. I encouraged others to read. I make others read a book in order to work for me.

I decided to write this book.

When I look back at my life of struggle, it set me up to work harder—many times harder than most people, at least in my perception. I also pulled some of that strength from reading. The books I've consumed help me adopt the mindset of not caring what others think, particularly when it comes not only to outside negativity but your own internal negativity.

Telling yourself every day that you're "less than" because you can't read gets tiring. I probably beat myself up telling myself that more than any of the negative words I heard about my difficulties from other people. When you can get past that negative self-talk and stop caring about what others say?

That's a powerful place to live.

NO NATURAL GIFTS

We have this misconception in our society that people with great success must be gifted or naturally talented. We only look at the positives in their life and completely gloss over their circumstances before their success—what it really took for them to get where they are.

Shaquiem Griffin is the first one-handed player to be drafted into the NFL. He had a deformity at birth that required his hand to be amputated. Do you think that having that meant he was blessed with a natural talent to play football? Of course not.

People with different abilities—not disabilities—have to work harder than anyone just to get what others perceive as average success. If you're starting behind the pack, you have to work harder than anyone else just to get to so-called normal.

This is why I say: Embrace the struggle. It creates

an appreciation that wouldn't be there if it came so easily. It creates a strength that others never get the opportunity to develop, especially if they have a natural talent that gets them their success. Never working for it means never appreciating it. Look more closely at the people who have really made it. They all have one thing in common—relentless grit and determination, especially in the face of adversity. They did not let the odds defy them—they defied the odds.

If you are the parent of a child who is struggling with reading, do not remove the struggle. While it might alleviate some pain in the short term, they will not be better for it. I know, as a parent myself, that when your child is hurting, you will move mountains to help them. Be mindful in helping them not to hinder them. Help them find their superpower out of their weakness.

I don't believe in natural talent. I believe people are born to a certain set of circumstances, and it's what they do with those circumstances that either makes them great or they are forgotten to history.

I've mentioned before that the history of literacy is important—that there was a time when it was ensured that information contained in books was inaccessible to the masses. It was only available to the elites or those in power. The Nazis burned books in World War II to prevent the spread of "dangerous ideas." Native American culture and language was almost taken away by acts of Congress in US history. That struggle is in my DNA. Knowing that history motivates me even further to not only continue my improvement in reading but to help others do so as well.

Struggle can be used for self-improvement, much like turning your weakness into a superpower. My personal struggle made me who I am today. I'm compassionate towards those who are disadvantaged and disenfranchised—those born into a world they never would have chosen for themselves. My answer isn't just to throw money at it, though that's not to say I think less of those who lend financial help to those who need it.

The way in which I can best help others is to share my story. Empower others to make positive changes in their life using my example to inspire and motivate. When my friend told me about Richard Branson's dyslexia and later, when I saw the fake Cambridge study, it lit a fire in me to keep reading. Just because someone is born into a certain circumstance doesn't mean they can't find a way out. Sometimes, though, they need the right kind of push.

LEGACY PLAY

Wishing for something won't make it happen. You have to want things and make them happen.

When I asked for God to take my life in his hands to do what he would and then my father passed, I realized that I needed not to ask for anything of anyone else anymore. I needed to make something of myself and to help others do the same. If there is one kid who picks up this book; if one parent passes on just one story from this that helps a child read; if one adult is listening to this as an audiobook and finds inspiration in any of the examples here, then I have done what I was meant to do. That's my legacy play.

I know for certain that I wouldn't be the person I am today without my struggle. If all of this had been easy for me, I can honestly say I don't know who I'd be today. I do feel, though, that my creator had a journey in mind for me. Though I was unable to read, he gave me the ability to think about things differently than most people. Even when my challenges were at their greatest, when things felt like they were at their worst, I always believed I had it in me to change the world.

My role models were business titans—those who

defined the American dream of rags to riches—those who came to this country with nothing or were born poor but worked at it for many years and never gave up on their dreams. Their stories—their legacy—gave me the drive and inspiration I needed to achieve the success I have.

There will be times when you or your child might believe they cannot achieve—that they will never be any better than they are now with reading. It is in that moment that you must continue to push them. That will be *your* legacy play.

I read once about what happens to the next generation of families who have or acquire great wealth. What happens more often than not is that the next generation loses. They don't have the same level of financial means because they are not taught to have ambition. It was important to me to teach my children ambition. I didn't want them to lose it, even as I built multiple businesses. I didn't want them to be spoiled.

I didn't want them to lose.

As such, I don't make their lives easy. My daughter asked me later in life why I made her struggle so much. She can see now at her age that everything

I did was so that she could be the person she is today. There were times when it was hard to watch her cry in frustration, knowing I could help her, but I needed her to think outside the box, same as her father had to. If things had been easy for me, I would have made it easy for her.

That's not the legacy I want to leave behind. Legacy to me is what is remembered when you pass on.

The only way to build wealth is slowly over time.

The only way to learn to read well is slowly over time.

Practice. Fail. Learn. Get up and do it again. Don't blame others for the problem. Keep working no matter how small the steps—no matter how small the gains.

Ripples make waves.

As the parent of a child with these struggles, you must start reading more yourself. Show your children how often you read. Your example will inspire them. On the other side, if you struggle, ask for help. Either one of these actions is the pebble in the pond—the ripple that flows into others to create big change from small ones.

CONVERSATION WITH YOUR FUTURE SELF

To calm myself on those nights I spent crying, wishing I could read, I'd imagine a conversation with my future self. I'd ask him what I did to get where I was in his time. Would he come back and give me the secrets to success?

Unfortunately, my future self never showed up. However, if I could go back in time and talk to my younger self, this is what I would tell him. I hope this example will help you talk to your children.

Keep grinding away, even if it doesn't make sense to you right now. Keep looking up those words you don't know. Continue to think about your problems in a different way in order to find that solution that no one has taught you. It's okay if you have to work harder than everyone else around you. You will inspire others who haven't read in years to pick up a book. You will teach others despite the fact that you hate school. You will be able to digest entire books one day, and you will be able to speed read. You will find the answers to your struggles by reading, and then reading some more.

All of this work will one day pay off, and you will look back and say, "I faked it until I made it."

Tell your children to imagine what it would be like to be successful on the other side of all of this. Seeing yourself as the best version of yourself can be incredibly motivating, as long as you never forget that the path to get there won't be easy, and it shouldn't be.

The ego is a funny thing. It can be easily bruised, and on this journey, make no mistake, it will be. There will be people in the way of your future self who will make you feel less than, who will make you angry, and who will make you question whether or not all of this is worth it.

I kept a quote taped above my desk for many years. It was a constant reminder to keep going in the face of doubt, whether it was that of others or my own. It came from Mark Twain, and I keep this saying close to my heart, almost like a mantra that I repeat to myself every day.

"A person who won't read has no advantage over one who can't read."

Whenever the journey seems too much, come back to this phrase. Keep it close to *your* heart and know that as long as you continue to put in the work, no one born with the ability to read is better than you.

Remember that, and there's no doubt that I'll see you on the other side.

CONCLUSION

A Promise Fulfilled

In the introduction, I told you that I wrote this book because of a promise I made.

I've always preached about the importance of having backup plans. It is impossible to predict the many situations you will encounter in life, and not all of them will be happy. Pain will come.

When people in my life pass away, I think of the impact and the lasting legacy. There were lessons taught when they were alive that I needed to heed, especially now that they are gone. My great-grandmother passed away many years ago. She taught me how to save money. She grew up in the

Great Depression and taught me how to plan for the future. When my grandmother died, I remembered how she loved unconditionally. She had many step-grandchildren, but she never loved them any differently than her flesh and blood. When my father died, he taught me how to live. His death led me to all of my discoveries about reading books dealing with overcoming difficulties, such as the books *Man's Search for Meaning* and *The Power of Now*.

Legacy plays a big part in my life now. Live the life that allows you to be a part of someone else's book. You never know what kind of impact you will have on someone else. A series of failures led me to successfully completing this book for those who can't yet read. I felt I owed it to readers to finish what I started because every book I've read contributed to my becoming the person I am today.

When I got the call from my oldest daughter that she was pregnant, she already had so many worries. She thought I was going to kick her out of the house she rented from me. Having learned from my losses and having struggled enough myself, I embraced her and told her everything would be fine. We grew closer through her pregnancy and I was happy to become a grandpa—I even bought a grandpa hat. Karisi Christina Gower became my "Power of Now" baby. I experienced every moment in the moment and got to embrace the now with her.

Every year, I take a trip back to Hawaii, where my father was killed. While there, I read books and reflect on life and try to find more meaning in it. One month after Karisi was born, I took all of my kids, their boyfriends, and the baby to Hawaii. As I held Karisi in my arms on the beach, I experienced the Power of Now, and I was a changed person for it.

When she slept in the bungalow, I would listen to my audiobooks. I listened to *Never Lose a Customer Again* by Joey Coleman. In his book, he gave me the solution to finish *my* book. I decided that I wanted everyone to feel the joy I felt there on vacation, living in the moment with my family. I stood over Karisi as she slept and thought to myself, *I am going to finish this book for you. I want my legacy to live on in my grandchildren. I need to help people, and I am going to finish it.*

I assembled the best team ever to help me finish the book. I actually booked a call with the company while I was on the beach. Scribe Media was going to be the answer to finishing this project. I was excited when I returned from vacation. I was full of energy and was ready to get the book off to an amazing start.

Just a few weeks later, early in the morning, I got the call no one wants to receive.

My ex-wife called me, hysterical, and told me that Karisi wasn't breathing, and that I had to get over to her house right away. I raced to my daughter's home and was the first one there. My daughter and Karisi's father stood in shock as the fire department and paramedics attempted to revive her. I was in the Now for every moment of it, including when they took her tiny body and placed her in the back of the ambulance. My daughter and I got into my car, and I told her, "I am not going to put anything out into the universe. I am just in the Now."

It was surreal, following them to the hospital, walking into the emergency room and seeing all the doctors and nurses surrounding her. The moment they told my daughter that her daughter passed away, I was overcome by waves of emotions, angry at life's unfairness.

What hope is there when there is no hope? What is the meaning of life when life is gone? I had a unique set of circumstances that led me on a path of self-discovery where I read books on grief and loss to deal with my father's passing, but none of it prepared me for this. I thought about the cause and effect of my decisions, and how they put me there for my daughter in her darkest hour.

Make no mistake, I wanted to quit the book when Karisi died. I told myself that it didn't mean anything anymore. But I made the promise to her. Every book I had ever read in the last few years led me to the ultimate understanding of Now. The time is now—don't waste it. This book no longer became my legacy. That belongs to Karisi now.

Her legacy will be this book.

YOUR LEGACY

My ask of you, whether you're the parent passing on this message, or if you're listening to this book yourself, is to get up each day with just a little more grit and determination than the day before. Find a book and start reading, whatever that means to you. Become a better person for it by learning about the experiences of others.

I want to hear your story. I want to hear your struggle and how you overcame it. I want to hear what books impacted you, and I want to hear your career goals. If you don't have something to work towards, then what are you doing with your life?

Go to willtalksbiz.com and contact me. I want to hear it all.

Even if you don't tell me your story, tell someone. Go and impact others. You never know how big of a difference you can make in someone's life, in the briefest encounter. Someone who only existed in my life for two months had a more profound impact than anyone else I've ever known.

Let's replace the illiteracy epidemic with a reading epidemic. That's not a bad legacy to leave.

A PARTING GIFT

When I set out to write this book, I did a bit of research to see if there were other books like it. There were some that were individual stories of business people, or physicians, or mothers telling a story to their child, but none of them focused on offering any kind of solution to the reader.

There are also books that exist for and by academics that dive into the science of reading disabilities. These books can be helpful, of course, to parents trying to understand their child's disability. However, with all of the books out there, there were few that highlighted the importance of the struggle, not just the why's and how's.

That is what I hope this book is for you. I appreciate that you have taken the journey to make it through this book with me. I hope you can take lessons and inspiration not just from my successes but my failures.

Understand that despite your challenges with reading, you have a superpower inside you waiting to be released. It's not about talent; it's about putting in the work. Read with a purpose. Read for your dreams. Read for where you are and where you want to be. Read for your future self.

If you continue to tell yourself you can't, you're going to find out you're right.

Most book conclusions tend to sum things up, but I want to do something a little different.

I want to tell you about some of the books that provided me with the greatest influence on my journey. I always want to know what the great leaders are reading. If I ever got to speak to someone who influenced my life or an author of one of my favorite books, I would ask them about which books changed their life—what book tops the list; what book are they currently reading, and why?

I want to give my list to you. It is my way of saying thank you, not only to you, but to the authors who wrote them. It is my hope that they discover what their books have meant to me and that they will provide you with the same inspiration that I took from them.

The 48 Laws of Power by Robert Greene. This was my go-to book any time I felt under a lot of pressure, whether it was at work, or life in general. I've been told by a number of people that the book is controversial and not to recommend it, but as with anything in life, you can only make that decision for yourself.

Shoe Dog by Phil Knight. I could not put this book down. By the creator of Nike, this one is just incredible. Believe me when I tell you that it is not just a business book. The story of his life is truly amazing, and I would recommend it to anyone.

In Order to Live: A North Korean Girl's Journey to Freedom by Yeonmi Park. A lot of times when I'm speaking to youth groups, I tell them, "You weren't born in North Korea, so you're lucky." Park was born in North Korea and defected to China where she was essentially a slave for many years and then broke free. The story details her journey to America, and it is one that I fell in love with. Many tears with this book.

I Can't Make This Up: Life Lessons by Kevin Hart. I love to laugh, and this book takes care of that while teaching at the same time.

The Dyslexic Advantage: Unlocking the Hidden Potential of the Dyslexic Brain by Brock L. Eide, M.D., M.A. and Fernette F. Eide, M.D., and *The Gift of Dyslexia: Why Some of the Smartest People Can't Read...And How They Can Learn* by Ronald D. Davis. If your kids are struggling and you think they might have dyslexia, these are the top two books I recommend. They dive deep into the tactical side of dealing with dyslexia. If you think after reading this book that you or your child or loved one is dyslexic, these books in physical or eBook form must be your next purchase.

How to Win Friends and Influence People by Dale Carnegie. This is a book I physically read on planes, chapter by chapter. I've used the content to disarm angry employees over the years. I've even suggested it to people in the middle of an argument when they're being particularly nasty because I know they haven't read it and they should.

The Power of Now: A Guide to Spiritual Enlightenment by Eckhart Tolle and *Man's Search for Meaning* by Viktor Frankl. Talk about changing your mindset. I was on vacation and still dealing with my father's death. Reading those two books made something happen. The themes of survival in Frankl's book, coupled with the idea that now is all you have in Tolle's helped bring in to focus that this is the only existence we have, and we'd better do something with it.

Letting Go: The Pathway of Surrender by David R. Hawkins. If you're not as into the spiritual side of things, this book gets into the psychological approach of being in the moment. Hawkins discusses how your mind can dictate a lot of the things that happen to your body and how to take control of that.

You Are Not So Smart: Why You Have Too Many Friends on Facebook, Why Your Memory Is Mostly Fiction, and 46 Other Ways You're Deluding Yourself and *You Are Now Less Dumb: How to Conquer Mob Mentality, How to Buy Happiness, and All the Other*

Ways to Outsmart Yourself both by David McRaney. Reading these books, I realized that every human has their own way of looking at the world and that our memories mess with us. When we look back on our memories, we play them differently in our head. How many fights have we been in because we remembered something differently, either from how it actually happened or from the way another person remembered it? We trick ourselves into a lot of incorrect thinking, and this book helps check that.

The Customer Rules: The 39 Essential Rules for Delivering Sensational Service by Lee Cockerell. This is the book I make everyone read to get a job in my companies. It follows Cockerell's journey from the customer service industry all the way to an executive at Disney World. He dropped out of college and used customer service to advance his career. You can see why I found him inspirational. You will find he has several other books, and I would recommend them as well.

Verbal Judo: The Gentle Art of Persuasion by George Thompson. For those in security positions or frontline customer service, this book will help you with de-escalation skills that may one day save your life.

*Unfu*k Yourself: Get Out of Your Head and into Your*

Life by Gary John Bishop; *The Subtle Art of Not Giving a F*ck: A Counterintuitive Approach to Living a Good Life* by Mark Manson; *You Are a Badass®: How to Stop Doubting Your Greatness and Start Living an Awesome Life* by Jen Sincero; *The Obstacle Is the Way: The Timeless Art of Turning Trials into Triumph* by Ryan Holiday. I've listed all of these books together as they all had roughly the same effect on me—to make me realize that the things you think are blocks in the road are actually opportunities and openings to a better you.

The 5 Love Languages: The Secret to Love that Lasts by Gary Chapman. One of the members on my team at the Tony Robbins seminar talked about this one frequently. It helped me have better relationships all around, and I recommend it for any couple.

All of Malcolm Gladwell's books. All of them. Seriously. I binge-read all his books back-to-back.

The 10X Rule: The Only Difference Between Success and Failure by Grant Cardone. I used this with my employees for a while to motivate them—to get them to do all things ten times harder.

The Bulletproof Diet: Lose Up to a Pound a Day, Reclaim Energy and Focus, Upgrade Your Life by

Dave Asprey, and *The Whole30: The 30-Day Guide to Total Health and Food Freedom* by Melissa Hartwig and Dallas Hartwig. These two books motivated me to lose weight as well as to close up one of my tobacco shops to open a health food store. It was a motivator to be the change I wanted to see in the world. That move actually got me a call from Asprey, which motivated me even further.

Relentless: From Great to Unstoppable by Tim Grover and *Grit: The Power of Passion* by Angela Duckworth. In his book, Grover discusses coaching Michael Jordan. These are both fantastic books about not giving up.

Why Didn't They Teach Me This In School by Cary Siegel. He wrote about money lessons that took me my entire life to learn.

And finally *Think and Grow Rich* by Napoleon Hill because it was recommended to me by B.G. Thank you, man, for all of your encouragement the day I told you I couldn't read.

Happy reading (or listening)!

ABOUT THE AUTHOR

WILLIAM MANZANARES is a successful serial entrepreneur, born and raised in the Tacoma/Puyallup area of Washington State. He is an active member of the Puyallup Tribe of Indians. Since 2005, William has been operating successful smoke shops and convenience stores in the area. In 2007, he opened his first restaurant and bar. In 2013, he opened his latest smoke shop brand, "Smokin' Willy's," on property that he converted to tribal trust property using the fee-to-trust process on his reservation. William continues to expand his business and is passionate about helping other natives develop their own tribal businesses and the tribal community in general.

Will's drive for success comes from the discovery at an early age that he was unable to read. Utilizing self-taught strategies, he has become a voracious consumer of books and shares his passion for them through community outreach, particularly to his tribe and the youth in his area. He even requires all job applicants with his company to read a book before consideration for employment.

Will is a sought-after motivational and educational speaker. Contact him at willtalksbiz.com.

Made in the USA
Middletown, DE
30 June 2020

10518845R00076